I AM ABOUT TO *lick* YOUR HUMAN

I AM ABOUT TO lick YOUR HUMAN

KATE PULLEN

Hardie Grant

BOOKS

INTRODUCTION

Four years ago, a girl brought home an
English staffy. Vince – otherwise known as Vinnie,
Vin, Vincenzo, Vincent or Vinaroo – has, like so many
other dogs, brought joy, laughter and disgusting
situations involving poo into the life of his owner, Kate.
He has also licked many, many humans.

As a fresh new dog parent, Kate did all the dog
parent things: puppy school, early socialisation, vet
visits and An Introduction in How to Speak to Other
Dog Mums and Dads at the Dog Park (online course).
Soon enough she was no longer known as Kate but
rather as 'that girl with the cute blue pup who loves to
say hello but won't stand still long enough for you to
pat him'. That is where this whole book began, and it's
taken both dog and owner on a bit of a whirlwind.
(Okay, let's be real, it's really just been a whirlwind for Kate.
Vinnie is living the high life, full of tuna and sweet potato.)

Did Kate ever think she'd end up creating a book based
solely on her love of these beautiful four-legged creatures
that we humans simply do not deserve? No way, she was
too busy disinfecting her hands. But here we are.

DOGS!

DOGS

doggos

DOGS

DOGS

What Are We Learning Today?

BINGO!

 SIT

FETCH

DROP

COME BACK WHEN CALLED

ROLL

 SHAKE

"I really do enjoy reading the business section of the newspaper before I urinate on it. It's important to remain current... and regular."

Henry, Great Dane, Aged 14.

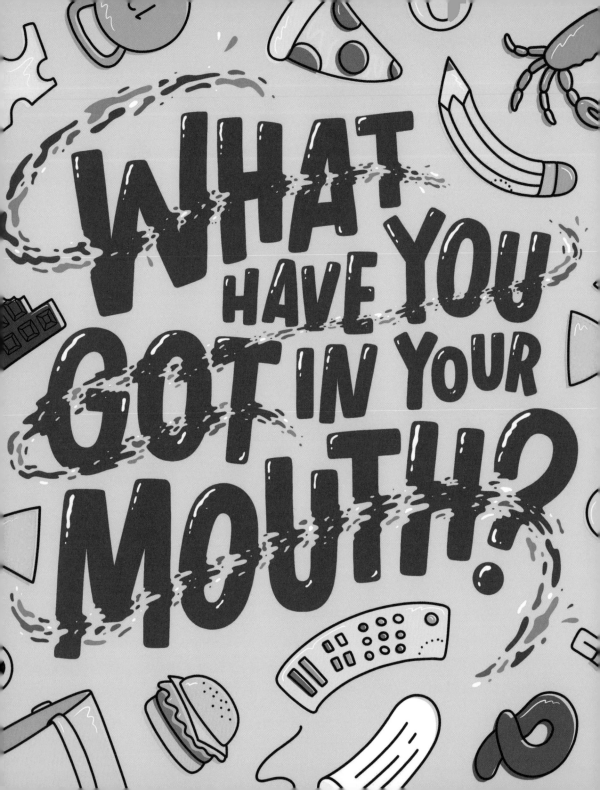

WHENEVER I DROP FOOD ON THE FLOOR, I DON'T BOTHER PICKING IT UP 'CAUSE I KNOW I'VE GOT A LIVING FLOOR CLEANER.

"I'M NOT SLEEPING, I'M MEDITATING. AND THIS SUNNY SPOT RIGHT HERE IS BEST FOR CLARITY."

Charlie, British Bulldog, Aged 7

Bizarre-yet-loveable Dog Moves

THE Cushion Sleep

SUPER CUTE LEG HANGING OFF THE SIDE

BLISSFUL EXPRESSION BECAUSE HE KNOWS HE'S WON AT LIFE

TAKING UP JUST ENOUGH COUCH THAT NO ONE ELSE CAN FIT

THE COMFORT OF THE HUMAN COUCH IS SIMPLY NOT ENOUGH

MUST BE AT LEAST TWO CUSHIONS

THINGS I'VE PULLED OUT OF MY DOG'S MOUTH...

ALL OF THE REALLY GOOD, ORGANIC

CORN CHIPS

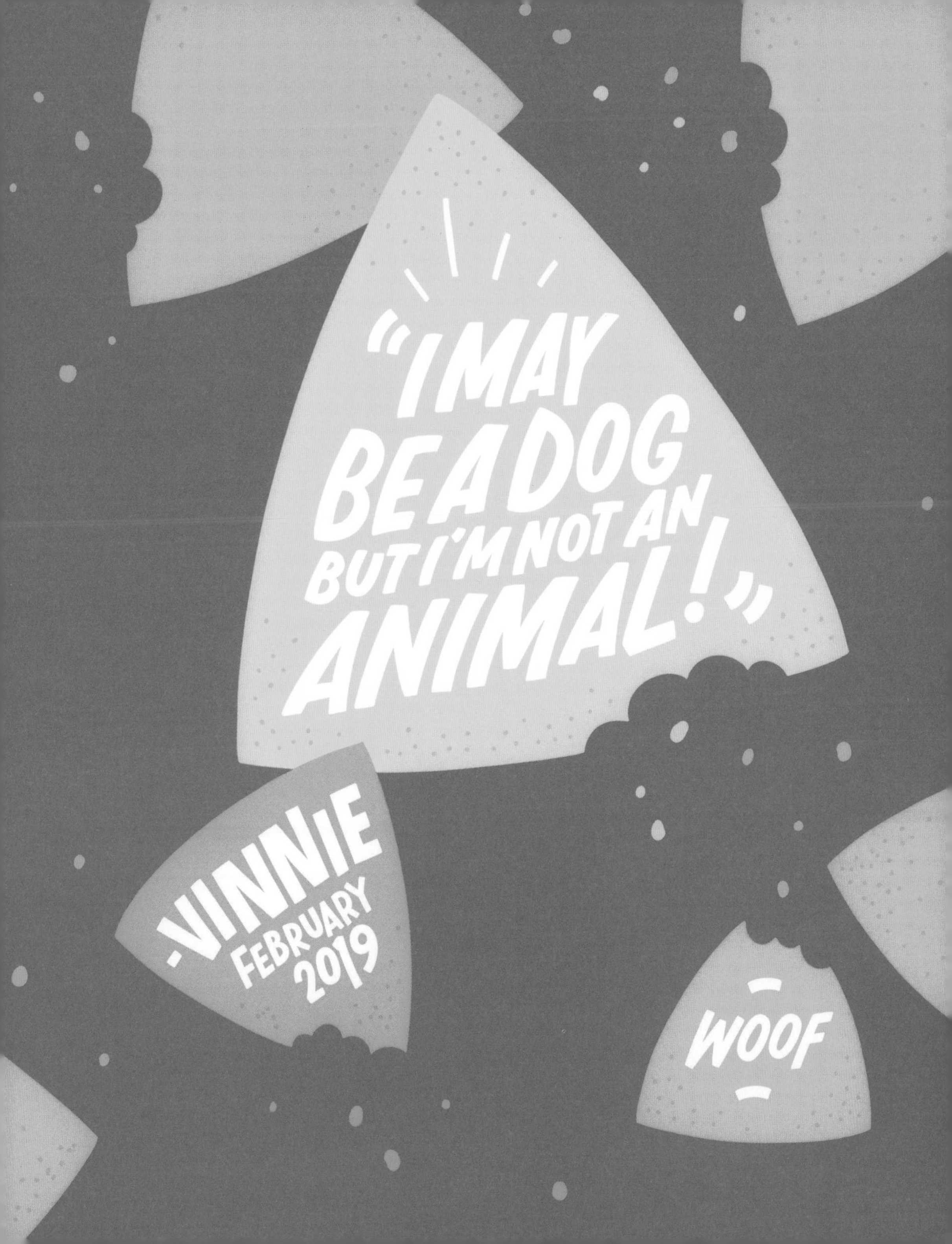
"I MAY BE A DOG BUT I'M NOT AN ANIMAL!"
- VINNIE
FEBRUARY 2019
WOOF

AN INTERVIEW WITH

EDDIE

AND HIS HUMANS

FULL NAME:
EESKUJULIK EDUARDO ENNO
(EESKUJULIK MEANS 'EXEMPLARY' IN ESTONIAN)

INSTAGRAM:
@EDDIETHERETRIEVER

AGE: 2

BREED:
NOVA SCOTIA DUCK TOLLING RETRIEVER

NICKNAMES:
EEDU AND PEEDU

STRANGEST HABIT:
HE'S KIND OF SCARED OF TRASH BAGS

FAVOURITE TOY:
A SQUEAKY, SOFT SNAKE NAMED USS ('WORM')

BEST DOGGO BFF:
HIS BROTHER SIMBA

MOST HUMAN TRAIT:
HE IS VERY EXPRESSIVE WITH HIS EYES AND BODY LANGUAGE, SO YOU CAN TELL REALLY EASILY WHAT HE'S FEELING.

HOME:
ESTONIA

MY DOG GOES TO DAYCARE & HIS REPORT CARD IS STUCK TO THE FRIDGE.

NAME: Vinnie

AGE: 3

BREED: ENGLISH STAFFY

CUTE SMILES

🐾🐾🐾🐾🐾

FETCH TALENT

🎾🎾 ○ ○ ○

KISSING ABILITY

♥♥♥♥♥ ·

LISTENING SKILLS

● ● ● ○ ○

EXCITEMENT LEVELS

⚡⚡⚡⚡⚡⚡⚡⚡⚡

TOP *Student!*

COMMENTS

We love having Vin! His best friend is George & he LOVES to sit on everybody's lap! He has so much love, but sometimes he just needs to make sure he listens nice & carefully.

WHAT KIND OF UNIMAGINABLE SMELL JUST ERUPTED FROM YOUR BOTTOM?

"I THOUGHT WE WAS BEING FOLLOWED BY A LAB A COUPLA BLOCKS BACK BUT I DONE A LOOP OF DA PARK AND I THINK WE GOOD. ALL DEM YUM TREATS FOR ME, PLS.."

Ellie, Weimaraner, Aged 6 months

THE UNEXPECTED UPCHUCK

MARCH 14

A Selection of spews

JUNE 3

THE CHUNKY CHUNDER

MARCH 8

THE ROCKET RALPH

APRIL 13

AUGUST 10

SEPTEMBER 2

THE PROJECTILE PUKE

THE REGRETFUL REGURGITATION

NOVEMBER 8

¡HUZZAH!

ATE IT STRAIGHT BACK UP AGAIN...

THINGS I'M PRETTY SURE MY DOG IS THINKING

I JUST DON'T KNOW WHAT TO TELL YOU, MA. YES, THE SANDWICH WAS THERE WHEN YOU LEFT BUT THEN TWO OR THREE POSSUMS ABSEILED ONTO THE BALCONY, CUT OPEN THE DOOR WITH. A. LASER. AND JUST ATE IT RIGHT UP!

An interview with

TOFU

and his humans

HOME:
AUSTRALIA

FULL NAME:
TOFU PUDDING JONES

COOLEST TRICK:
CAN SEE A LOAF OF BREAD THROUGH 4 METRES of CONCRETE

AGE:
3

FAVOURITE TOY:
ANYTHING WITH A SQUEAKER

BREED:
SHIBA INU

FAVOURITE ACTIVITY:
GOING TO THE BEACH

FAVOURITE TV SHOW:
POKÉMON

MOST HUMAN TRAIT:
LAZINESS

INSTAGRAM:
@TOFUPUPPER

things I've pulled out of my dog's mouth ...

LEG OF THE LIVING ROOM COUCH

DOGS I LIKE TO PAT:

big dogs

sleeping dogs

fast dogs

old dogs

fluffy dogs

dogs THAT ARE A little plump

tiny dogs

puppy dogs

"I LOVE MY HUMAN BUT HE REALLY NEEDS HELP WITH HIS INBOX. WHERE IS THE FILING SYSTEM HERE?"

Lilo, Papillon, Aged 9

THINGS I'VE PULLED OUT OF MY DOG'S MOUTH...

UNIDENTIFIED OBJECT ON THE SIDE OF THE ROAD

EWWW

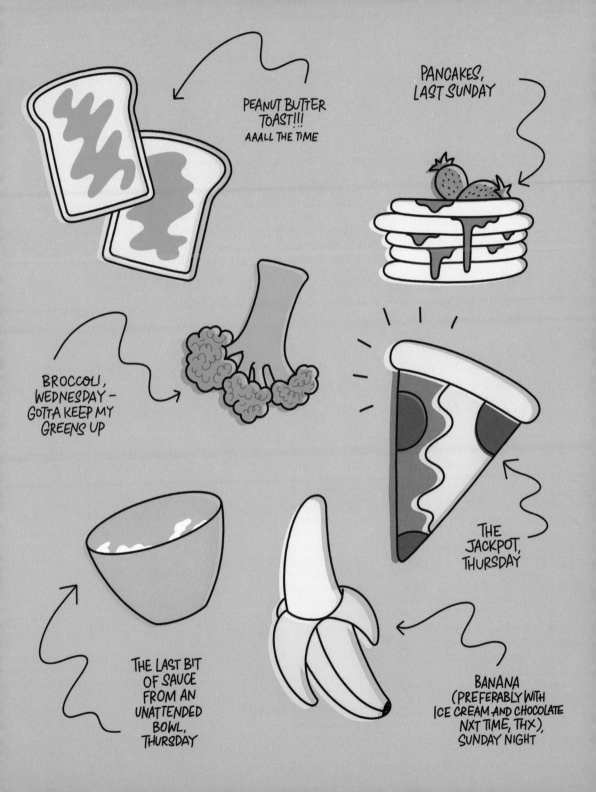

zip

zilch

ZERO!

...said no dog owner ever

What Are We Learning Today?

BINGO!

PLAY DEAD

VACUUM IN PEACE

WAIT FOR DINNER

GRAHAM

WALK WITHOUT PULLING

HIGH FIVE

WEE ON COMMAND

All OF THE DOGS I HAVE Met:

TUESDAY

THINGS I'VE
PULLED OUT OF
MY DOG'S MOUTH...

· A ·

TAMPON

TAKEN FROM THE

BATHROOM

BIN AND

SHREDDED

IT WAS PRETTY GROSS

SOMETIMES
I TAKE MY DOG
TO PARTIES
SO I KNOW I'LL
HAVE SOMEONE
TO TALK TO.

"Dooo you have a ball? Pretty sure I see a ball! Go on, throw the ball! BALL!"

FRED, FRENCH BULLDOG, AGED 1

FOIL-WRAPPED PIZZA

STOLEN FROM THE BENCH AND SWALLOWED WHOLE

IF YOU SEE A DOG,

and don't pat the dog,

WAS THERE ACTUALLY

ever really a dog?

"OHHH HEY!
HI! HI! HELLOOO!
YOU LOOK NICE!
OOO SO NICE!
GREAT HAIR!
WANNA HUG?"

Buddy. Boxer. Aged 4

THINGS I'VE PULLED OUT OF MY DOG'S MOUTH...

A BALL SO SLOBBERY IT MADE IT INTO THE GUINNESS BOOK OF RECORDS*

*IT DIDN'T, BUT IT REALLY COULD HAVE

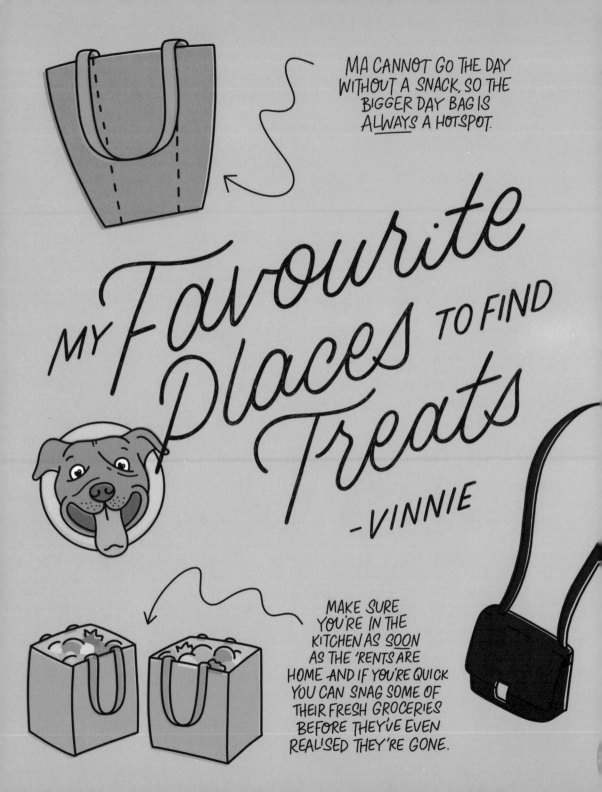

MA CANNOT GO THE DAY WITHOUT A SNACK, SO THE BIGGER DAY BAG IS <u>ALWAYS</u> A HOTSPOT.

My Favourite Places TO FIND Treats

-VINNIE

MAKE SURE YOU'RE IN THE KITCHEN AS SOON AS THE 'RENTS ARE HOME AND IF YOU'RE QUICK YOU CAN SNAG SOME OF THEIR FRESH GROCERIES BEFORE THEY'VE EVEN REALISED THEY'RE GONE.

MY MENTOR BOB'S MOTTO WAS 'ALWAYS CHECK THE POCKETS'. SMART GUY, THAT BOB.

DEPENDS WHO'S BEEN WATCHING TV LAST BUT BE VIGILANT, 'CAUSE BEHIND THE COUCH CUSHIONS COULD DEFINITELY BE A WINNER.

YOU HAVE TO BE LUCKY WITH THIS ONE. THERE'S NOT ALWAYS TREASURE, BUT AS I ALWAYS SAY, 'NO SNIFF, NO SUCCESS!'

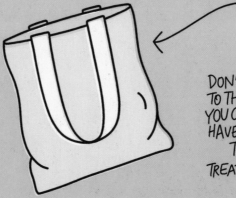

DON'T LISTEN TO THE HATERS, YOU CAN NEVER HAVE TOO MANY TOTES!

TREATS ABOUND!

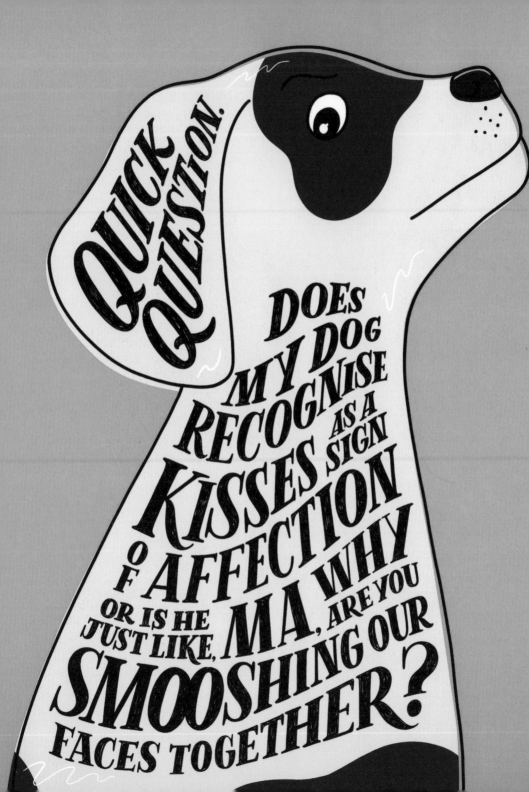

My dog eats better than I do

An interview with **TUNA** and his humans

BREED:
CHIWEENIE

INSTAGRAM:
@TUNAMELTSMYHEART

NICKNAMES:
TOONEY, TOONS, TUTUS, MACOW, BABY, PRINCE (AMONG OTHERS)

BEST DOGGO BFF:
CURRENTLY TAKING APPLICATIONS!

WEIRDEST TRICK:
IF YOU CLAP YOUR HANDS AND SLAP YOUR LEGS TO A SPECIFIC BEAT, TUNA FETCHES HIS FAVOURITE TOY, COLIN.

AGE:
9

ADOPTION STORY:
TUNA WAS ORIGINALLY JUST MEANT TO BE A FOSTER, BUT WHEN HE & HIS MA, COURTNEY, MET, THEY REALISED THEY WERE FOREVER.

MOST HUMAN TRAIT:
CRABBINESS, SPECIFICALLY IN THE MORNING

FAVOURITE PLACE TO SLEEP:
IN HIS HUMAN'S BED, UNDER THE COVERS

FAVOURITE GAME:
PLAYING FETCH WITH HIS TOYS

What Fun Are We Having Today?

BINGO!

PORTRAITS

BURYING BONES IN THE HOUSE

BIRTHDAY BASH

ACROBATICS

INSTA ACCOUNT

NEW WARDROBE

YOUR **DOG OWNER** CHECKLIST

The Lifestyle Edition

ABILITY to locate ALL the DOG-FRIENDLY CAFES

Puppuccino

INSTA ACCOUNT dedicated TO YOUR DOG and their EXPLOITS

VARIOUS DISGUISES to help SNEAK your DOG into WORK

YEAH!

FRIENDS with dogs so you can organise SUPER CUTE PUPPY PLAYDATES

VARIETY of LEADS & COLLARS to suit ANY OCCASION

Wet WIPES

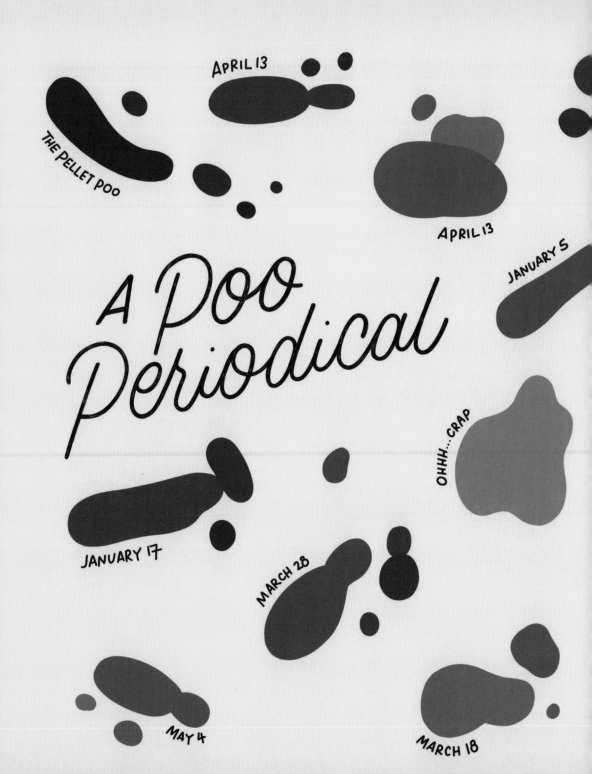

A Poo Periodical

APRIL 13

THE PELLET POO

APRIL 13

JANUARY 5

OHHH...CRAP

JANUARY 17

MARCH 28

MAY 4

MARCH 18

JUNE 30

... OOPS

APRIL 14

FEBRUARY 24

FEBRUARY 22

JANUARY 17

APRIL 3

APRIL 13

APRIL 5

THE SWEET POTATO POO

JUNE 6

"It's Friday and tbh I've just been hanging out for a wine in the bath."

Ralph, Labrador, Aged 8

HIS OWN LEAD

Our thoughts go out to all the tennis balls lost to the park, the beach, the next door neighbour's yard the spot behind the couch no one can reach, the back of the cat, the excited puppy down the road

"MAGGIE HERE, REPORTING FOR DUTY. KIDS ARE OFF TO SCHOOL. DISHWASHER IS ON. NOW FOR THOSE BELLY RUBS I WAS PROMISED."

Maggie, German Shepherd, Aged 10

All OF THE DOGS I HAVE MET:

SUNDAY

CHERYL,
SITTING (AND SNOOZING)
ON HER OWNER'S LAP

TULLY,
JUST WANTING
A PLAY AT
THE PARK

BUTTERCUP,
HANGING OUTSIDE
THE FARMERS' MARKET

BENTLEY,
OUT ON A
MORNING WALK

CHARLIE,
WAITING PATIENTLY
FOR A PAT AT
THE PARK

THINGS I'VE PULLED OUT OF MY DOG'S MOUTH...

NAPPY LEFT IN THE MIDDLE OF THE ROAD AND FULL TO THE BRIM

anyone else like the corn chip smell of their dog's feet?

asking for a friend

"YES, A HOMEMADE CASSEROLE IS GREAT, BUT

DON'T TELL MA I JUST REALLY LOVE TO EAT MY OWN POO!"

John, Golden Retriever, Aged 3 months

* NAMES HAVE BEEN CHANGED TO PROTECT THE PRIVACY OF INDIVIDUALS

Things I've Pulled Out of My Dog's Mouth…

KITCHEN SPONGE

CORNER SWALLOWED WHOLE!

CAME OUT THE OTHER END!

HE'S NOW GREAT AT CLEANING BENCHES!

BINGO!

HIDE AND SEEK

DOGGO BFF

BEST KISSER

BAWSE PATIENT

GOOD PASSENGER

BATH WITHOUT FUSS

WAIT. THEY'RE THE SHOES YOU WEAR WHEN WE'RE GOING FOR a... OMG WE'RE GOING FOR A walk!!

I'M SORRY, YOU WANT ME TO GO OUTSIDE AND PEE IN THE RAIN?! IS THAT WHAT YOU'RE SAYING TO ME RIGHT NOW?

INSTAGRAM:
@ASPENTHEMOUNTAINPUP

AGE:
7

BREED:
GOLDEN RETRIEVER

MOST HUMAN TRAIT:
HE LOOKS AT YOU DIRECTLY IN THE EYES & HE ALSO SMILES!

HOME:
COLORADO

NICKNAMES:
BUDDY. BUBBA. ASPY. ASPERS

STRANGEST HABIT:
HE LIKES TO PUT HIS HEAD UNDER WATER TO GRAB ROCKS FROM RIVERS.

HE WILL DO IT FOR HOURS!

FAVOURITE ACTIVITY:
HE IS OBSESSED WITH CHIPS & ICE SO PROBABLY SOMETHING TO DO WITH EITHER OF THOSE THINGS!

FAVOURITE PLACE TO GO EXPLORING:
AS LONG AS HE CAN BE OFF LEASH, IN A RIVER OR SNOW, OR AROUND PEOPLE. HE IS HAPPY!

FAVOURITE PLACE TO SLEEP:
CUDDLED UP IN BED WITH HIS HUMANS

I tuck my dog into bed every night

ENTIRE

STRING WRAPPINGS

of a

CHRISTMAS TURKEY

VOMITED ON THE DOOR-MAT

IN THE

EARLY HOURS

of

BOXING DAY

MY Favourite Cheese

TYPES OF

—VINNIE

THAT ONE WITH ALL THE HOLES IN IT

THE CHEESE IN TINY, TINY STRIPS

(you really need a lot of these.)

MMM THAT SUPER DELISH WHITE STUFF THAT IS SURELY ACTUAL CLOUDS FROM HEAVEN

"TRAINER'S BEEN UPPING THE REPS LATELY. IT'S A KILLER BUT I'VE REALLY BEEN NAILING FETCH AS A RESULT."

Patty, Jack Russell, Aged 2½

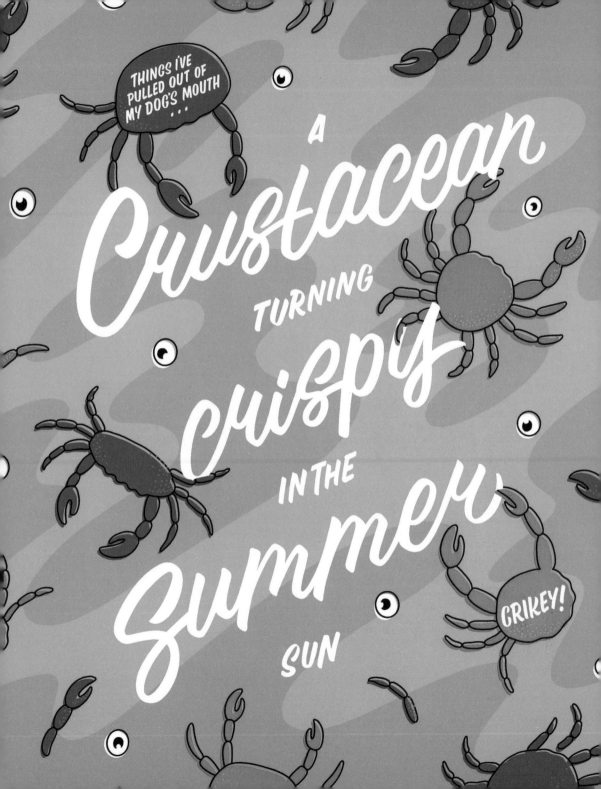

WHY WOULD YOU EAT THAT?!
GROSS
HANG ON, IS THAT... POO?!
WOT
OHHH NO
EWWW

WHAT HAVE YOU EATEN?
UMMM
LEAVE IT
OUT! OUT!
WHAT'S IN YOUR MOUTH?
NO

"Best blowout in the City PLUS liver treats on arrival!"

BABS, BREED UNKNOWN, APPROX. AGED 2

KINDA-GROSS-YET-LOVEABLE DOG MOVES

THE Sliding OF THE Bones

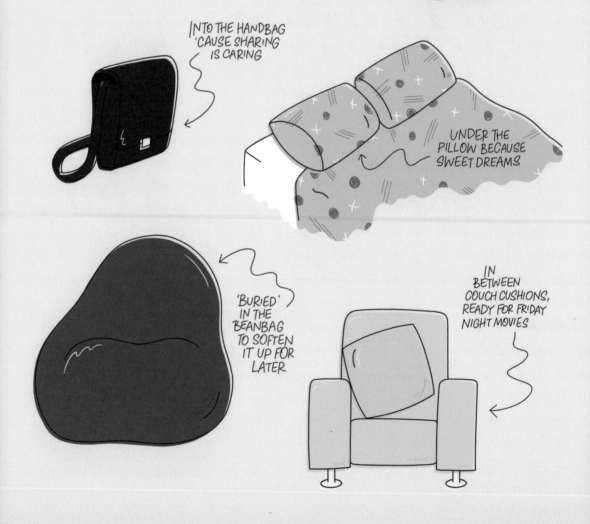

INTO THE HANDBAG 'CAUSE SHARING IS CARING

UNDER THE PILLOW BECAUSE SWEET DREAMS

'BURIED' IN THE BEANBAG TO SOFTEN IT UP FOR LATER

IN BETWEEN COUCH CUSHIONS, READY FOR FRIDAY NIGHT MOVIES

THINGS I'VE PULLED OUT OF MY DOG'S MOUTH...

A
Block
- of -
dark, dark
chocolate

Retrieved in the form of vomit at the vet.

MUCH drool, such HAPPY.

WORLD, why am I so BEAUTIFUL?

We must all BOW TO THE one AND only CHICKEN ROLL.

Coming soon, in pieces, to a living room near you

REMOTE

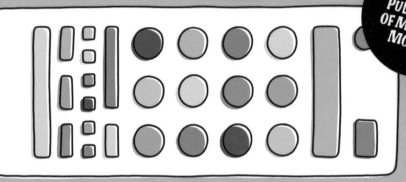

THINGS I'VE PULLED OUT OF MY DOG'S MOUTH...

CONTROL

"A STAR EFFORT, WE'VE NOT SEEN DAMAGE LIKE THIS BEFORE!"

- Samsung staff member

★★★

"WHAT A SET OF CHOMPERS!"

-Proud vet

★★★★

"SUCH A GOOD BOY, HE PASSED ALL OF THE BUTTONS!"

- dog walker

★★★

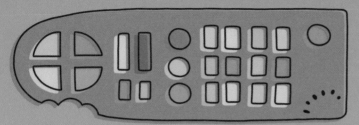
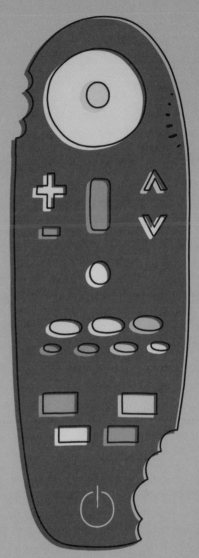
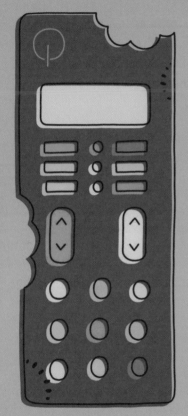

THINGS I'VE PULLED OUT OF MY DOG'S MOUTH...

MY MATE MEL'S LUNCH STOLEN FROM HER DESK WHEN SHE WASN'T LOOKING & VOMITED ON THE OFFICE CARPET 30 SECONDS LATER

"The name's Barry but my friends call me B·Dizzle!"

BARRY, PUG, AGED 1·5

THINGS I'VE PULLED OUT OF MY DOG'S MOUTH...

What Are We Doing Today?

BINGO!

PAWDICURE

PUPPY SCHOOL

BEACH TRIP

ROAD TRIP

PUPPUCCINO

DAYCARE

THE INITIAL

Sketches

FOR THIS

book

An interview with

CAPTAIN

and his humans

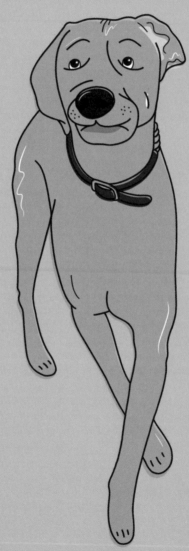

BREED:
WEIMARANER

HOME:
AUSTRALIA

AGE:
5

INSTAGRAM:
@TOMANDCAPTAIN
@STICKSANDCAPTAIN

WEIRDEST TRICK:
GREETS EVERYONE AT THE DOOR, WHICH ISN'T UNUSUAL EXCEPT THAT HE LITERALLY WON'T LET THEM IN UNLESS THEY GIVE HIM SOMETHING: A COMPUTER, HANDBAG, CAR KEYS, FRUIT, MAIL, MILK... ANYTHING HE CAN HOLD OR DRAG TO THE KITCHEN, WHERE HE DROPS IT AFTER DOING A FEW PROUD LAPS OF THE HALLWAY.

FAVOURITE TOY:
A LARGE KIWI. HE CARRIES IT AROUND AND JUST HOLDS IT IN HIS MOUTH. YOU CAN SAY 'WHERE'S YOUR KIWI?' & HE WILL SEARCH THE HOUSE & RETURN A HAPPY, PROUD DOG WITH HIS KIWI.

STRANGEST HABIT:
LOVES EATING FULL LEMONS. HE WILL DROP A STICK AND UPGRADE TO A LEMON IF HE SEES ONE IN THE GUTTER.

FAVOURITE PLACE TO SLEEP:
IN THE HUMAN BED UNDER THE COVERS

FUNNY-AND-LOVEABLE DOG MOVES

THE Resting Positions

PRIMO RELAXO. ON BACK AND, FOR EXTRA CUTE POINTS, CROSSED FEET.

CHIN MUST ALWAYS HAVE THE OPTION OF EXTRA SUPPORT.

PLACED ON MULTIPLE LEVELS, JUST TO MAKE SURE ALL BASES ARE COVERED.

I MEAN,
NICE BUM, BUT
SURELY THIS ISN'T
COMFORTABLE.

BALL IS CLOSE BY,
JUST SO THAT THEY KNOW
THAT YOU KNOW, THAT
PLAY IS AN OPTION
WHENEVER YOU'RE READY.
WHENEEEEVER YOU'RE READY.

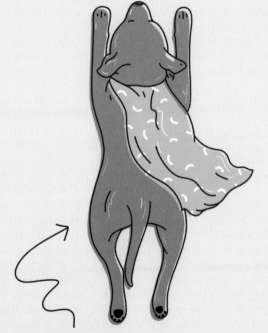

THE WEIRDEST
AND CUTEST FROG
LEGS I EVER DID SEE.

INTRODUCING...
SUPER DOG!
(CAPE OPTIONAL).

"WRESTLING. BALL. BREAKFAST BURRITOS. AFTERNOONS IN DA SUN. MUCH BELLY RUBS. PIZZA. AND FRIENDS. AND PIZZA.

YEP. THEY'RE PROBABLY MY *favourite things*."

VINNIE, ENGLISH STAFFY, AGED 4

MEET *the* ~~DOG LADY~~ Author

Kate Pullen

Kate Pullen is a Melbourne-based illustrator and letterer
who can't drink caffeine, making her choice of profession
and home city seriously questionable.

When it comes to creating, Kate's aim is pretty simple:
use images and letters to communicate a message that
makes people happy. And when her English staffy,
Vince, came into the picture, it opened up a whole world
of new content she wanted to create and share.

If it isn't clear already, Kate loves dogs.
Exhibit A: these 128 pages entirely dedicated to their exploits.
When not patting, walking, talking about or drawing dogs,
she also enjoys the admittedly odd mix of true crime
podcasts and incredibly upbeat musicals.

Published in 2020 by Hardie Grant Books,
an imprint of Hardie Grant Publishing

Hardie Grant Books (Melbourne)
Building 1, 658 Church Street
Richmond, Victoria 3121

Hardie Grant Books (London)
5th & 6th Floors
52-54 Southwark Street
London SE1 1UN

hardiegrantbooks.com

A catalogue record for this
book is available from the
National Library of Australia

I Am About to Lick Your Human
ISBN 978 1 74379 581 1

10 9 8 7 6 5 4 3 2 1

Publisher: Pam Brewster
Editor: Emily Hart
Design Manager: Jessica Lowe
Designer: Mietta Yans
Production Manager: Todd Rechner

Colour reproduction by Splitting Image Colour Studio
Printed in China by Leo Paper Products LTD.

A big thank you to the Hardie Grant team,
Emily, Pam, Mietta and Jessica,
for helping spread my love of dogs.

Jes, thanks so much for your continual
guidance, support and pep texts.

My fam and friends who have looked
after Vin or listened to countless
stories about his antics.

Rusty, my biggest supporter, thank you
for always being in my corner.

Vin, I love you buddy.